Sonni's Abyss

Sonni's Abyss

✦

A Collection of Poetry

Mark A. Leon

Contributing Editors:

Raquel Soledad Avila
Christine C. Baker

iUniverse, Inc.
New York Bloomington Shanghai

Sonni's Abyss
A Collection of Poetry

iUniverse books may be ordered through booksellers or by contacting:

iUniverse
1663 Liberty Drive
Bloomington, IN 47403
www.iuniverse.com
1-800-Authors (1-800-288-4677)

Because of the dynamic nature of the Internet, any Web addresses or links contained in this book may have changed since publication and may no longer be valid.

The views expressed in this work are solely those of the author and do not necessarily reflect the views of the publisher, and the publisher hereby disclaims any responsibility for them.

ISBN: 978-0-595-52027-5 (pbk)
ISBN: 978-0-595-62117-0 (ebk)

Printed in the United States of America

To my Mother and Father, Sandra and Solomon
They are my true life teachers
Thank you for always believing in my talents

I would like thank those that have helped me achieve the goal of my first published works including, Rhonda, David, Howard, my parents, Bruce and Daniel, Kimberly V for being in my life for some many years and still my best friend, Sonni, the inspirational force behind the title and cover and my fellow world traveler, Jenny who taught me how to love, Kim and Annie who taught me how to commit to something, Raquel for proving you can make a spiritual connection that can transcend time, Brian, Michael and Neil and all of Tinsley 3 whom without them college would not have been the same, Rachelle, who could always see the good in others, Jake and Nicole who stuck with me through the bad times, Scott, for making all his life and career dreams a reality, the N.U.T.S. that taught me that life is a complete cycle of fulfillment, Dee for helping me get my life back in the right direction after I was excluded from society for so long, Will, who taught me not to give up on ambition not matter how long it takes, Jason for being my best friend growing up, Lad the dog no one will ever forget, Heather for giving me … you know, Maxine and Frank for welcoming us to the neighborhood and never walking away, and to everyone else that has impacted my life whether it was for years, a day or just an instant.

Contents

INTRODUCTION xi

Sonni's Abyss 1

- *Re-Birth* 2
- *Inner Strength* 3
- *Greatness* 4
- *Blind Innocence* 5
- *Oriental Blossom* 6
- *Remember* 7
- *Anyone Else* 8
- *Near But Gone* 9
- *Long Cry* 10
- *Peace In your Dreams* 11
- *Satin Breath* 12
- *Silent Yearning* 13
- *Misguided* 14
- *The Rising* 15
- *Alone* 16
- *Ideological Peace* 17
- *Voyeur* 19
- *Audience of One* 20
- *Wicked* 21
- *Friends in the Eyes of a Stranger* .22
- *Footsteps* 23
- *Uncovered* 24
- *Autumn Angel* 25

- *Life's Stage* *26*
- *Patriotic Fraud*. *27*
- *Fallen* *28*
- *Waiting Time*. *29*
- *Canvas*. *30*
- *Grounded*. *31*
- *Greed*. *32*
- *The Smile*. *33*
- *A Dream in the Clouds* *34*
- *Waiting on an Angel*. *35*
- *On A Clear Night You Can See Forever*. *36*
- *Breathless Tranquility*. *37*
- *Original Quotes* *38*
- *Amy 5* *40*
- *Jestine's Song* *41*
- *Melody of Life* *42*
- *The Decision* *43*
- *Life's Darkness* *44*
- *The Answer for Hope* *45*
- *Translucent Childhood* *46*
- *1, 2, 3* *47*
- *Untitled*. *49*
- *To Jessica, With Love* *50*
- *Across the Bar*. *51*
- *Passion*. *52*
- *For Ina* *53*
- *Destination Unknown: Ode to Life* *54*
- *Crippled*. *55*
- *Wedding Vows* *56*
- *Canvas of Water*. *57*
- *Eternal Encounter of Love*. *58*
- *The Guardian of Darkness* *59*

- *Love Lost* *60*
- *Heartbeat* *61*
- *Meet Me Halfway* *62*
- *Last Goodbye* *63*
- *Life's Dream* *64*
- *Empty Mirror* *65*
- *Dreaming Reality* *66*
- *Prophecy Retreat* *67*
- *The Flame* *68*
- *I'm Sorry.... For What?* *69*
- *Rest in Firenze* *70*
- *Hope and Faith* *71*
- *Social Love Affair* *72*
- *Ode to Travel* *73*
- *Two Worlds Apart* *74*
- *Valentine's Day to Amy* *75*
- *Grounded* *76*
- *Baby Blue* *77*
- *The Poet* *78*
- *Self Reflection* *79*
- *In Flight* *80*
- *Crashing Waves* *81*
- *Frozen Past* *82*
- *Temporary Goodbye* *83*

INTRODUCTION

It takes a very special soul,
to capture the emotions of man,
from happiness, to grief and love,
they number as many as the grains of sand,
which lie upon the vast shoreline,
where he walks to clear his head,
and there he finds inspiration,
for a beautiful poem instead.
On a clear night you can see forever.
He writes of sun and moon and stars,
and from the grassy knoll he lies upon,
of the eclipse and sparkling Mars.
He writes of nature's seasons,
their vast and wondrous display.
Where common man fails to see,
he finds the beauty in every day.
His writing became a passion,
for what his heart could not contain,
and as he shares his thoughts with you,
he is vulnerable once again.
With this vulnerability,
he reaches out for your hand,
for he wants to bring you happiness,
and help you to understand,
that if you want to live life fully,
you have to open up your heart,
take down the walls that divide you,
for we each are only a part,
of this diverse humanity,
which loves and hopes and grieves and dies,
and in his dream like poetry,
you shall be honestly surprised,
for in it lies a mirror,
reflecting the emotions of today,
things that you've felt in your heart,
with an emotion you could not convey,
for his is a special gift
he'll pull your dreams down off the shelf,
and as you get lost in Sonni's Abyss,
you just might find yourself.

—Jill Pendley

"Today is the only yesterday and tomorrow we will ever know"

—Mark A. Leon

Sonni's Abyss

Re-Birth

Read the words of writers and imagine it is you looking at yourself from inside the mirror behind your eyes hoping for a momentary escape from the fortress of your skin

Desperate for a promise

Walking the empty streets surrounded by thousands of faceless strangers so familiar in the song that is sung in your dreams

Feelings pray in your thoughts

What happened to the child that still looks to space and flys with the birds

Fate has aged faster than time will allow

Fire now brings chills home

A place never seen by the visible eyes covered all the days of life

A year is gift wrapped under a galaxy of life's tree waiting to be opened to the memories that hold the answers to future prizes of the heart

It is time to go to sleep and empty the thoughts of despair for droplets of innocence to drench the body and reinvigorate the soul

INNER STRENGTH

Where do we go now?

It may lead to the end of the beginning

It may bring us to a place inhabited by our worst fears

Fear is strength

It holds the destruction of grace on a podium sacrificing words of dead prophets in ancient hymns

Promises of eternal unification

Now is the only certainty that words cannot explain and thoughts cannot break

Destroy yesterday, forget tomorrow and wait for it

Open your eyes and see the moment with complete passion

Present the fury of fear with the hidden desire of love

GREATNESS

Life is the ordinary development of uncertainty

Each day is a clear explanation of the certainty that will not happen

Each page is pre-written by boys and girls living the dream of all dreams

Waiting for a moment, a time, a sign

Turn around, the followers are ahead now

Lead through the path cleared by history filled with gold and diamonds

Riches await the dreamer and dreams await the visionary that understands what we refuse to see

Believe the unbelievable

Achieve the unachievable

Be afraid of nothing but fearful of everything

We are the leaders but need not leadership

We must step into vines of poison for poison can be wisdom to the focused eye

Convince yourself of the desperation that creates a self inflicted world of mystical clarity

Tie the rope to the end of the cliff the hovers below your fortress of safety

If you want it, take it.

If you can see it, reach for it and hold it; don't ever be afraid to let go

BLIND INNOCENCE

Life is a variable reminder of what lies ahead

Ahead of the clouds that cover the skies

Ocean of the ocean that thunders below

Eyes of blue look down from the heavens

A child points up to a smile he can only see releasing a glow of humility in a desensitized society

We all run for a destination

We all pray for the hopeless

We all hope for the prayer that will answer the silent question written on the beds of our mind like a deal made by an atheist in the presence of the devil

We are hypocrites in a structured world

Dare to live but never live a dare

The journey south begins with the healing of broken wings from birds not yet born to a life not yet lived

Birth is a destination, naïve to the educated, confusing to the purest of knowledge; spelling lesions of life with blood dropping from the sky and spelling out the word of four ancestors for only the blindness of innocence to see

ORIENTAL BLOSSOM

Make love through song

Harmonies flow through your outstretched arms

Eyes of crystal radiance transcribe verses of centuries past bellowing in the chimes
of the morning bells

The artist brushes strokes of silky hair over the innocent curves of your smile

When your mind's made up only the soul can release the temptation of absence

Let the sky lead the birds to the coldest of all warmth

Led by the lost but safe from the humanity of humans

Through prayer; inspiration

Bow your heads to the silent heroine singing the lyrics of our deepest thoughts

Be one together holding a charm of hope shining a light through the darkness of
what lies ahead

REMEMBER

My will is gone but not forgotten

Like a runaway train, I am off the tracks and out of control

My soul is a runaway; living on the streets searching for a new meaning

Each sunrise deteriorates the spirit

Under the stars, the night protects this fragile pawn naked to a world controlled
by neglect and tortured hatred

Ignite a flame

Rekindle the light that awakened fondness

Remember the hugs; remember the smiles; remember the late night talks and
always a clear conscious when your head hits the pillow

The flame burns not for today but yesterday

It can't return to the comfort it once knew; but be comforted by the thoughts
represented by this light

ANYONE ELSE

Cut me and I will not bleed

Kill me and I will not die

Pillage me and I will not feel invaded

Fuck my soul and rape my dreams

My heart is a virgin on a cross bleeding for the sins of man

Too long I have cried

My tears too valuable to be wasted on hopeless reminders of mortality

Hope comes in a paper bag filled with temporary reminders of happiness

Have I been dealt the right eye for my sinful regression?

My eye is blind to the sight of the living spirit that left my side so many sunrises ago

Pages on the wall turn with the wind

Time continues in slow motion

Someone talk to me but don't say a word in my presence

I wish I was anyone but me; anywhere but here

I keep running out of time

I woke up today dead but still breathing the air of the living

NEAR BUT GONE

Dreaming away the night protected by the darkness that places a blanket over my fears

I am soothed by the familiar thoughts of a mother sitting next to my ailing soul holding my hand and putting a sea of peaceful waves into the corners of my mind

Lying on a bed of stones crushing the pores of my tortured body taken over by a death filmed in slow motion and repeated over and over in the theater inside my head

Each memory played in rewind until the blood covers my body and drips away what I cannot forget

I am drenched in a past that is tattooed in my memory with poisoned ink

Serving as a permanent reminder of my inability to reach out and return the same protection that provided security all my life

Now I am alone but always surrounded by the ghosts of a past that will never die

I look up, she is there

I look down, not too clear

To the left she appears; to the right nightmares aware

I close my eyes and with each second of darkness a million thoughts of visual agony formulate

It is a utopia of inner destruction taking over my body one moment at a time and never to stop until ashes remain

LONG CRY

She called out for help only to be heard by the gates of hell

Raped of her sense; a burial in her mind

The numbness feels so good

It is the ecstasy of my self loathing void

I'll see you around when around dissolves the memories of life

Bleed with me through the walls that hold me captive

Scream the kettle tune as it boils over in my veins

Wake to the past of a single rose; a single visitor on the knees of the earth that bares us and now shelters this eternal home

PEACE IN YOUR DREAMS

Can you hear me calling for I have not said a word

I reach for your beauty only to catch the air that we share apart

Release your thoughts through the timeless look in your eyes

Open your heart but don't let me in

A smile captivated in the clouds

A glow radiating from the setting sun

My mouth is blind, my eyes are speechless

Bittersweet dreams, my only reminder of a beauty only to be seen by the guardian angels protecting the clouds

Time pauses for you as the flowers sing your song of harmony and hope

You are words of wisdom unspoken; dreams unfulfilled

You are a glimmer in time whose memory will last a lifetime

Hold your dreams close and hopes closer for the chimes of life ring a new song echoing your names to the heavens

Behold a vision, but for a second never to be forgotten

SATIN BREATH

Under her breath, as she sleeps voices of angels sing

Protected over a cloud of prayer, chimes ring to the sounds of forefathers of generations past

Like porcelain, the finely sculpted curves of her body rest in motion with only the sounds of silence to protect her from the thoughts that bellow in her heart

Tonight the gates of clarity open its path shadowed by uncertainty and wonder

She is one, mother and daughter; shared souls walk together

Under a bed of satin, the breath of two become one. Time freezes a picture of purity captured in innocence transcended in the poetry of hope

Submerged in clear blue waters, the skies open its blanked and wrap them into a journey above the heavens

SILENT YEARNING

Her silence tears me up inside

The burning innocence in her eyes yearn to call out

A barrier of forbidden love releases its prowess

They reach out for a connection; but denied the word of the heart

We wait in breathless ambition

MISGUIDED

Misguided innocence murdered in broad daylight

Darkness warms our fears with an enchanting aroma of tropical mango from the decaying remains in time

It is in our hearts we pray

It is with our mouths we rejoice in song

Two words etched in stone deep in the caves of fallen legend

Leaders perished

Villains rose above the law of man drenching their hands in the holy water of immortality

Forever laughing with each cry of death

Reborn in metal and rebuilt in a stone mountain of steel; one by one a new layer has tendered to its destiny

Under a blanket of sharp knives glass is cut into a razor sharp cross of lust

Power-stricken desire swallows the edges leaving behind charity and vision to unlock the key to tomorrow

THE RISING

I heard you screaming deep in the corner of my brain

My heart pounding with each murmur of conscious doubt

Healthy vibrations resonate on the sick terrain of a land of lost love

A cloud of hope covers the imagination of the immaculate child sheltered by the
womb of protected time

She kissed away the last grain of sand sunk deep inside the desert in my eyes

Smoke rises from my ashes

Life begins with a flame lit by the promise of a new beginning

ALONE

I can see the light of heaven

I can feel the fire of hell

I crawl for the first time yet I have not been born

A finger snaps and life has passed leaving behind a permanent reminder of what
will soon be forgotten

Resting on the tombstone a rainbow of flowers wilting away from the passing of
months of cold and darkness

I sit alone surrounded by ghosts chained to their eternal resting place

Comforted by the silent whistling of wind I rest my spirit above the ground that
will soon take me as its own

I'm at peace with my future

Born alone, live alone, die alone

IDEOLOGICAL PEACE

From a bar not distant from our own, a lonely man showered in intellectual uncertainty

A drink is poured; a smile shared

Fondness of a momentary companionship to be shared

A stare, a sip, a gaze of agreement for a word never spoken

The sun sends shadows over the glisten of newly polished wine glasses

With a single lure, the impending conversation begins; the magic of disagreement forces the tide

Debate ensures as two candidates stare into the view of visually omitted audience

Realism and ideology hold swords at arm's length preparing for battle. The blood of an innocent army of children is poured over the plains of our future

The fight continues another day but the glass is empty

The candidates retreat with the setting sun; a new day, a new strategy awaits

VOYEUR

An angled glance of unintentional voyeurism formulates the embrace of two hands sharing the security of one space

A brush of the hair, a kiss on the cheek, a head on the shoulder

The motion picture in my head is plotting out the stabilization of the notion of a modern romantic scenario

A kiss covers the tracks of an elusive affair not to be revealed to the main character

The action will disguise a pain

She shared body of the wicked soul; the voyeur knows

The lie is the clarity of the truth to the unflawed observer

Five feet, two minds, two stories.... yet one truth

AUDIENCE OF ONE

The scorching sun plays strings of fire

Descending clouds color the fields of grey

Harmonious whistles blow off the coast to be settled into peaceful obscurity

With a leap of faith, the earth rises; trees soar

Birds deliver the messages castaway by the sea

Present arms as the followers continue on the unknown path with the omnipotent leader hidden from the mortal eyes

The sinners sell innocence for profit; hearts on the ground lay peacefully to rest

WICKED

Running toward the shine of a soft moment of glorious paradise

Never stopping for the truth along the path

Words disguised as feelings playing off the lips of deception

Oh, this time it is real on the stones of false promises

The glass hides the images of emotions bleeding in silence and flowing down the cracks in the perfect pathway

Can you see the ghost recite absolute proverbs hiding under a costume designed by the demons we created with time?

We are all chasing shadows trying to buy a life only on loan to us from the heavenly spirits

The epilogue will read that life was a failure in a world where success is a cliché of desperation blinded in a euphemism of children reciting the words of teachers trying to main innocence as long as the rains of aging hold back

Compassion hold tight as inexperience grows to hate and hate to awareness to denial of the infinite end

The sun sets on another quiescent day and all is at peace for the moments we rest our wicked minds

FRIENDS IN THE EYES OF A STRANGER

Heads down to the ground questioning a life taken by ignorance

A shot in the night, a community torn

Reborn to uncertainty

The sun rises to one less child

Soaring above the wings of peace; forever a symbol

Together strangers rejoice in sorrow

The sky beckons an opening shining on the circle of wasted memories

Below she rests

One bullet, millions of shattered dreams flow in a stream of blood

FOOTSTEPS

Footsteps reminisce in a pool of eyes watching from the edge of insanity

Thousands of messages float to the surface drowning from the ears of loneliness to salvage cries of suicidal peace

Bubbles of isolation; hugs of disparity; calls of silence

Gravity lifts off the plains of balance

A long wet morning of solitude drenches the desert of wine making the shepherds drunk on madness

Footsteps washed away by the demons laughing inside

UNCOVERED

A melody but a shadow harmonizing in the corner of my mind

Strings of light play for an ensemble of lucent thoughts

Bellowed beneath the inner security locked in a box of frozen time

Chimes a note written in permanent ink of memories

Wild beasts of envy thirst for self preservation in the heartland covered in sands of history

Dust storms shield generations past but always to be uncovered for a repeat performance

A little boy finds a stone

A general lays to rest

A nation born to certain demise

AUTUMN ANGEL

Beautiful, beautiful, beautiful

Auburn moonlight touched from the grace of chiseled stone

The artistry of imagination paints colors of subtle perfection

In the eyes a hint of yearning; each beat a reminder of a gift that is the spirit of the soul

Fingers outstretched in thought

Time passing before the night sky

The touch of the silky lining of the skin hints of jasmine

Clarity a halo hovering above her guided soul

Alone she is surrounded by a world opening its eyes for the first time

LIFE'S STAGE

I saw you yesterday hypnotizing my emotional frailty like a circle in the wall spin-
ning away from my mind

Writers and prophets tattoo forever a moment in time etched into the foundation
of compassionate retreat

The words spray painted in our minds; dripping of blood from the crying chil-
dren of yesterday

Home is a friend in need when the need of friendship is the glue holding us apart
from a puzzle that has no end

Chimes of the passing seconds erase; now leaving only memories hidden over our
shoulder in the distance

We retreat to the safety of danger awakened by life and frightened by the notion
of accepting our existence wrapped in the cornerstone of realistic fantasy

Dream away your life; live out your dreams

Tomorrow is the only way to hold on to yesterday

Act one, life begins and ... action

PATRIOTIC FRAUD

Whistling, I hear lines of poetic verse coating the walls of polyphonic euphoria

The headlines read of a new tomorrow crippled by the media that holds our hands through the jungle of societal bliss

My life hanging on a string of symbolic emails read by strangers bidding my bones to the pioneers of glutton and waste

Wearing my blood soaked tears on the mantle of an unfinished monument with faceless names and a cause void of meaning

Victory is only a corruption to the writers who feed us a luxurious meal of make believe

Radicalism at home is peace in a foreign land

Don't wake up because the nightmare only begins if you open your eyes to the world that has left you behind

Toys replaced with guns and innocence but a tagline for the misfortune growing in your stomach

Faces of soldiers branded on the greenbacks of the American Dream

We are caught chasing a finish line with no end and no memory of a beginning

FALLEN

I want to see the farm that raised that young woman in the picture

The colorless still that was to become the spiritual guide I call mom

The woman that rescued me from fetal animosity and now sleeps beside a bed of clouds

I'm waiting for you, innocent to the reality that distances you from me

New life sits in your chair warm from the comfort of yesterday

My kisses vanish into an image of a young girl lying in a bed of flowers holding onto her dreams

Through the door I walk tall with my head to the ground

Stopping for a moment I look to the stars and carve a prayer to the ears of angels with wings to heaven

It's time to rest my tired soul and close my heart for one more long night

I want to stop falling

WAITING TIME

Are we looking for something right before our blind eyes?

Am I running to or from a wave of love destroying the past and cleansing the path to the future?

Waste is time bottled up in the distance of our minds

I walk alone with you by my side

Empty streets remind me of the steps imbedded in our life's journey

In the darkness and silence of uncertainty the battle ensues

Blood will be shed and sacrifices made with a vision of victory hailing in the clouds of a new tomorrow

Take my hand and let me be your hero

CANVAS

In a damp corner lying alone drowning in emptiness, I surrender to your dreams

You make sense in a world disillusioned by life

Harvesting the fruits of canvas

Painting strokes of emotional color penetrating within the pores of time, a heavenly form takes shape

A signature of hope documents a burning desire for unrequited completeness distant from the outstretched brush extended from my lifeless hand

GROUNDED

Bitterness hangs in the threshold of the valley of fear

Betrayed by trust and held close by the virtues of the virtuous song of the relic servants of the word

Scriptures bleed on the clothe of the pure spirits flooding the temple of self doubt

Let the light of inspiration shower flames of mindless abandon into the cave of broken hearts

Hallucinations provide clarity to a world only known by the survivors of the holocaust of terror ringing high above the extended hand of lady liberty

The skies are empty but for a cloud of dust swimming for the freedom of a new tomorrow

Helplessness floating below with signs of salvation elevating from the core of frozen heat

The morning air has washed away

Purple skies give away to blue in a shower of rainbow glistening from droplets high above the face of clouds

Our chariot glides through air breathlessly following a path of destiny set by the forefathers of centuries past

Past and future have come together

Cobblestone roads, a reminder of the path ahead

GREED

Greed, a power we cannot control

Deep within the heartland of an untamed being, it grows like a cancer without fury

Home exists only by name

Conquest, a tool for salvation, comforts the beast on its quiet journey

Penetrating the skin, piercing the pulse of all sanity, it swallows the pit of tranquil intelligence

Echoes of emptiness pulsate from every direction

Each beginning must put to death a new end

We are guilty of other's crimes

Jails are walls we call home

We pledge our loves to the golden spirits decorating the inner core of the castle

True love but mere words written by poets of centuries old acting out a truth so few can see

Breath in the freedom confined to a small box expanding slowly with every passing of the sun's sky

Be thankful for the gifts you never have

Destroy the unattainable pleasures pressuring the conscience mind

Greed is growing now

Close your eyes and hide

THE SMILE

Droplets fall from the blossoming rose

Falling to the embrace of a nourishing bed of nature's gift

Beyond its appearance is but a sign; a truth held firm by the guardians of the golden scroll of life

Deeper and deeper it reaches in the depths of eternity

It continues to flow further and further from the ears of our spirit

Listen close as its sound swallows our fears

It opens up our suspended reality and awakes the sense of the mystical beings

Be true to the one ... be one with the truth

Open up ... be free ... let go of the one you love and love will let you free

A DREAM IN THE CLOUDS

Can you hear me through the voice in my eyes?

In my heart I am brave, in my silence a coward

With a glance I am blind by a pureness that surrounds your beauty

Holding a truth inside is but a shelter releasing a desire for passionate innocence

Is the fire in my eyes?

With each look, my thundering silence grows stronger

Screaming the words only angels will hear

Your hair a salvation

Your hand a guide

Your radiance the answer to questions yet to be asked

For a moment your castle became mine and mine yours

Built on a foundation with the strength of stallions

Yet broken by the wind of silence

WAITING ON AN ANGEL

The end provides a fortitude of innocence bleeding through the guilt of hearts worn by the passing of a moment

Defined by the actions shed by the fears

We wash away the tears buried in the memories recorded in the back of our minds

Tomorrow her beauty will catch your eye and fade into a fresh white coat of shy exhilaration

The reality of a future together will disappear in a dream filled with magic and mystery

You are beautiful

Your soul floats above a sea of dead passion

You will always be the love never found; the redemption never seen

A new year

A lost love

ON A CLEAR NIGHT YOU CAN SEE FOREVER

There is no greater feeling than the touch of the wind off the ocean front brushing against your face. The smell of the fresh ocean waters fills your nostrils with a sense of home. The touch of the water as the wave crashes on the soft sand reminds you of a refreshing glimmer of wet magic. The same ocean that drips from your skin can also swallow you up alive with its terror. It is a powerful force full of mercy and despair. Warriors have conquered the high seas, explorers have chartered its path but the simple man who feels the true emotions and vision of its beauty can look to the skies, clear their eyes and inhale the breathless majesty it holds

As I walk down the shoreline, my feet soak in the gentle sand crystals and cover my feet with its gift. I leave behind a trail, one that will soon be washed away cleared for the next fortunate souls that bear their heart to the mother ocean

BREATHLESS TRANQUILITY

Lay me to sleep my eternal angel

Protect me and caress my soul with a bed of gentle passion

My heart has been captured

You are a thief in the night and you have magically stolen my soul

Beneath the heavens lies an illuminated spirit with eyes of ocean blue

A smile that can only be expressed by the pure of heart

An inner beauty that showers rose petals over a dark empty field

It was always you

Forget me not for you are the stars that fill my empty sky

The sun that shelters the earth

I am yours, heart, mind

ORIGINAL QUOTES

"Happiness is accepting that you can be alone"

"The heart is a sin covered by layers of protective innocence and a mask of undiscovered knowledge"

"Love is but a sacred vow made between two hearts"

"Nothing is more perfect than a clear sky together with the one you love"

"To expose the emotional hold on man's heart is the ultimate vulnerability"

"I can see now the destruction caused by a lonely heart"

"Nourishing the heart with care and respect breeds a healthy mind and soul"

"Once in a lifetime, a special someone comes along and from that moment on the world is a better place to live"

"The worst state of being is being in love"

"The stars shine above as the world lay to rest with the thoughts of dreams dancing in their heads"

"Love is an unexplainable act of foolishness"

"As we stare into the moonlight, the soft touch of your hand meets with me. We stare together into the infinite unknown as thoughts of sweet sensual kisses race through our heads"

"Fresh air is well worth the time spent outdoors"

"Children relinquish that youth we lost through maturity"

ORIGINAL QUOTES—CONTINUED

"I saw her standing alone in the mist. Her beauty filled the air with an aura of magic. Her silhouette in the darkness glowed like the stars up above. Her deep eyes mesmerized my inner soul. Though our hearts would never meet, this moment together would last forever"

"The pain of death is only felt by the living"

AMY 5

Close your eyes and lose yourself in the magic of the kiss

The bellowing swallows sing the morning song

The embrace of nature's gifts engulf the rejuvenated soul

He catches her eye

Her golden hair waves with the whistling trees

The sparkle in her eyes is sky blue

The skin is of renaissance beauty

Behold the sculpture; carved from life's hands

Alone she stands tall

She breathes my world

She possesses the key to my heart

Unlock the door and link the bridge from halfway, we will meet

JESTINE'S SONG

Guide me into your arms like a leaf finds its home under the earth's soil

By land I journey to your soul's gate; by air I dream of a magical journey into your fantasy

My hopes rest on a pillow made of lost memories hidden from the naked eye

Visions of heaven reflect through your eyes as words of poetry pour from your motionless mouth

Your lips hold the truth but never to be spoken

Your heart echoes with each beat answer to questions that have not been asked

We think a prayer, not to be thought

We dream a dream not to be dreamt

We speak of songs never to be spoken

We sing a lullaby that can never put us to rest

Why let our hearts call for the song of the songs, the prayer of the prayers, the peaceful lullaby

It is our heart together that will open the path to each other's locked world

The key to your dreams is with me

The lock to my heart is with you

Be free to ourselves and together we ourselves will be

MELODY OF LIFE

Can a tree feel the pain of a lost love?

Can a flower nurture its kin with the warmth and love of a mother's touch?

Can the soil feed the mouths of an innocent infant?

Can the rain cover the body of a lost soul who is searching for answers?

Can the snow cover the despair that fills that earth with cold fury and create a beauty only the heavens can know?

Do the roses provide a scent that can only be felt by the bond of lovers?

The willows whisper a song of silence as the wind supplies an orchestra of flutes and trumpets

An audience of nature's creatures fills the seats that mother earth gives us and listens to the angels sing a melody of hope

With each deep breath remember the gifts that surround you on the stage of life

THE DECISION

The bird flies free over the grassy knoll

Wings spread for the world to see

The sun, but an arm's length away alone in an empty sky

Walking alone; footprints left behind remind the ocean of its duty to cleanse the motherland

Genuine is the wall of stone built by the hands dripping in sweat and blood

A foundation of trust cemented in the courtroom of time

The jury has been selected and trial has commenced

The first witness, my childhood speaks of innocence and beauty, youth and vigor

The jury sympathizes

Next, despair, confusion and sin join the temple of adult reflection to burn away the bible of values held close by the inner child

The verdict is near but very far away

The clock ticks louder and louder into my ears screaming for mercy from a fate sealed away from only the heavenly gatekeepers to see

The air is thick

The children ponder the evidence on the playground laughing away the confusion leaving clarity and promise for tomorrow

In the distance a light rises from the cold sand patch

I wait in rejoice as I cry in silence

LIFE'S DARKNESS

Black is your mystery

Darkness is your strength

Light burns through the solitary enchantment penetrated deep within a forest of thought

A spell is blown in the dust of time; oceans crash and rivers flow into an abyss of infinite destiny

Shattered dreams reveal hope in a time of disillusionment

Broken glass tiptoeing through grains of fine sand lingering from a storm of silence

Sounds of fury scream only to be heard by no one

Infinity has found its end leaning on the edge of life's grave

Each grain falling six feet deep and a million miles below

Emptiness flows as the rivers meet and the skies and the calling can now be heard

THE ANSWER FOR HOPE

Do you love me?

Do you need me?

Do you yearn for my every touch?

Do you reach for me when I am not there?

Do you call me when you are in fear?

Do you hold my heart close to you?

Am I your home when you need salvation?

Am I your friend when your heart has no direction?

Am I your lover when your lips need a soft touch?

Am I your provider when you need shelter?

We are one separately, but we are two together

TRANSLUCENT CHILDHOOD

I know you're here in spirit watching over me with a tombstone hovering over my head

Your memory is dark

Don't watch me

My grieving has clouded my ideology of the pureness of your love

Be aware, my sins cry for forgiveness for death needs blame

Pain follows me two steps behind like a shadow following its owner to certain demise

Deep prose echo variances of familiar sounds of youth hidden in the backpacks of children only known by those on the other end of the mirror

Reflections in time remind me that my future is forgotten and my past paves a light ahead

I can feel myself inside the comfort of your rose petals

A sweet smell of caramel and lemon nectar invade my head hypnotizing the fruits of hope with an artist's rendition of home

Playful and wild; soft and safe; return to the shelter now transformed to darkness

1, 2, 3

#1

Dream the whispers of danger away

Feel the fragrance of life illuminate the sweet smell of nature

Alas, silence breaks through the wall; tranquility rests on bedside

We are one

The soul answers the prayer of the living

Unity rests in the mind

Freedom speaks in silent tones

Listen … the answer lies within

#2

Look deep … concentrate

The soul seeker is watching

The haunting image of light awaits

His power burns the haven inside

Hold tight, shield thy gate; resist the temptation

The heavenly brightness reaches out its hand

The peaceful beauty draws the inner child

The end is near

Thunder roars its final encore

#3

What I hold before me I cannot find the place

A simple piece of the puzzle

In shape and form it is quite normal yet has no home; no one to interlock with

Though its appearance is subtle, it holds all the answers

It is the most important element of the jigsaw of life

The heart knows no truth without the purpose and wisdom to guide us to a unified spirit

The puzzle rests on the mantle complete now

The pieces still maintain continuous flow for our destiny fluctuates upon the actions and desires of the imagination

UNTITLED

As I lie beneath the open sky the uncertainty that surrounds is illuminated by
heaven's light

Beautiful sounds fill my mind of a sweet lullaby

I close my eyes as I begin my plight

My life aches of an inner emptiness

Help me, dear Lord seek salvation

Open my heart to peace and happiness

The moment is seized by a vision

We are but a creation but each possesses a purpose

The answer lies within

It must be found to achieve eternal destination

I hold my hand secure to my heart…. I wait

To Jessica, With Love

Your words ring like a silhouette in the sand

Grains of tranquility rain like fire rushing through the trees to a destiny of ruin

The beat within holds back its sexy flame waiting for the rose to unlock its fury
captivated in love

Your weapon; your words

Your weakness; the unknown

Your fortress is protected by a distance undefined by man

Laughter breaks the barriers

Lust destroys the walls

Desire draws a path to you

Along its route a split

To the left forbidden passion; to the right a sun with two doors

A decision is held in the hands of the wise only to be viewed by the purest of
heart

ACROSS THE BAR

The sparkle of silver radiates from the gentleness of her fingers

Her eyes scream of confusion with every pure sound of harps resonating the echoes of angels singing hymns of love

The night air waits in breathlessness for the morning to arise

Two strangers stare into the emptiness across the table as thoughts, not to be spoken fill the air

Time is standing still as innocence disappears and emotion has taken over controlled thought

Their skin touches

Hearts race for a finish line not be found

Holding close to a moment each hopes will never end

The sun has conquered the evening stars; a new day has arrived

Now a dream created by the innocence of a kiss has come to an end

Today has become the tomorrow we hoped would never come

Remember the moment that took our hearts away as we stared from across the bar

PASSION

Can she possibly know the truth?

I am inside her now

Reaching into the abyss of untainted sexuality

Subtle curves pave the way to the impenetrable castle

Do not enter, the sign reads

Beware of the unspeakable truth cautions my deepest thoughts

Fueled by passion, driven by desire and warmed by a smile only to be seen by the true believer

She is the prize for a contest that does not exist

Where does it end?

Straight ahead, eternity clouds my vision

FOR INA

From the east, a journey to a new land

Mysterious hopes hidden in western dreams following a path void of glory

Family is pictured in your mind intoxicated by poisons surrounding you

From the distant morning clouds a voice of reason praises thoughts of poetic solitude

In despair, a ray of light shining through the gates of a new tomorrow

The stars, a point of reflection

Under one sky we are all one

Holding hands up to the infinite abyss and singing songs for all to hear

Millions of faceless bodies colliding searching for the grail of the complete heart

A daughter reaches for her mother over troubled waters creating a bridge of promise that cannot be broken

DESTINATION UNKNOWN: ODE TO LIFE

In flight we stand still, destination unknown

Onboard, the personification of a life's journey heading up to the heavens

Each level a plateau with a valley breathing not far behind

The higher we reach, the further we go; less we know

What is the purpose we call existence but a wavering cloud hovering below the energy that burns above and the lands that shelter us from the storm

Below we look up; above we look down

Yet no matter where we turn we are in the middle of the great abyss that has no beginning or end

In our pocket lies hope, sewn into the cloth that covers our fears

Faith is but a string, dangling off the thread that holds all of nature's mysteries in its web

If we escape, return we must not

If we remain, the voyage must end

We hold onto a future that has yet to arrive, but with it, memories of a past left behind

Backwards, we run on to move forward faster

Try to stand still and the ghost of time will capture you with its dark freeze

Where can we go from here; destination unknown

CRIPPLED

Whistling, I hear lines of poetic verse coating the walls of polyphonic euphoria

The headlines read of a new tomorrow crippled by the media that holds our hands through the jungle of societal bliss

My life hanging on a string of symbolic emails read by strangers bidding my bones to the pioneers of glutton and waste

Wearing my blood soaked tears on the mantle of an unfinished monument with faceless names and a cause void of meaning

Victory is only corruption to the writers who feed us a luxurious meal of make believe

Radicalism at home is peace in a foreign land

Don't wake up because the nightmare only begins if you open the eyes to the world that has left you behind

Toys replaced with guns and innocence but a tagline for the misfortune growing in your stomach

Faces of soldiers branded on the greenbacks of the American Dream

We are caught chasing a finish line with no end and no memory of a beginning

WEDDING VOWS

You came into my life like a warm breeze

As quickly as the sun rose, the sun settles on what seemed but a moment in time

You warmed my heart with you innocence

You soothed my soul with your gentle laughter

We traveled thousands of miles to find each other but always letting go

Maybe letting go was the only way I could realize how much I needed you

Life was always about me

I didn't need anyone; the road was my strength but that was only an illusion

The only truth now stands before me and completes the journey I have been on all my life

I found my home and that home is you.

CANVAS OF WATER

I reach out and rejoice in an ocean of passionate waves

The heart of the sea showered by rose petals taming the intensity of its domi-
nance on our weak spirit

Skies of grey

Seas of blue

Colors of abundance stimulate a rainbow of solitary tranquility

Wild flowers reach for Heaven revealing the smell of a newborn untainted by life

Grains of sand through my fingers return home spreading over the earth laying
the carpet for the idle explorer washed on the beach in search of a new home

Reflections of the sun, like a painting without a title, bring light to the ocean can-
vas

The wind is talking in verse, rhyming from the west; a poem of love that the
lonely fisherman, far from his land hears with his heart

The stars connect one by one

A puzzle with no end but a continuous beginning with new chapters written each
day

The sun is a storyteller and us its children

We sit back and listen to the words of our future not yet written

ETERNAL ENCOUNTER OF LOVE

Love is the essence of beauty

It is the inner most thoughts that warm our soul

It is the smile of innocence from a young child

It is the blossoming flower of a bright spring morning

The power of love prevails as sure as the stars shine from the heavenly skies

Help us, Dear Lord realize the true sign of endless peace and happiness known as love …

THE GUARDIAN OF DARKNESS

Feel me penetrate the surface of the moon watching over you and pulsating a glow that corrupts your body with illumination

Heat and passion run like waves hiding under the clouds

Tones of gray and blue coat the fields of darkness awakening from a deep sleep

The sun fills the night with magic

Steady confusion brings stability to chaotic silences screaming in our heads

Sounds of music from an organ buried with the soil of memories

Layers of past, present and future deafen the soft sounds of life falling deeper and deeper into the core of lava and flames

Each second, another year

Each year, a fallen leaf

Each sunrise, a longing for the night

Each baby christens a new beginning to an already established end

The guardian sleeps for his job is complete

The gates to the grave, a new home protected only by the light of eternal darkness

LOVE LOST

My heart stopped and the wind has blown its final gust

The symmetry of life is thrown off with the echo of a fleeting heart breaking over the rocks of time

Gather your thoughts and hold them tight in the box of memories hidden deep within the abyss of purgatory

Love is but an illusion covered in the horror of passing poets and dreamers, only to be buried inside the empty grave

Deep in the ground screams bellow through the rocks and the aches of generations of lost souls hoping for an escape from the eternal loneliness that has caged them

Can the sun shine again over an empty sky or has the fatal darkness taken hold of a lifeless world

One innocent symbol remains

Pure as the morning dew moistening the pillowing greens that color the ground

It calls for answers with no reply

It hollers for the truth to a question silenced by time

It holds a handful of emptiness disguised as hope

Love is lost but has never been found

Hell above and heavens below and in the middle fear of a happiness growing in the halls lit by darkness and illuminated by the blood of the sacrificed

The canyon holds a final resting place with a tomb yet to be inscribed

Looking down I see my future

HEARTBEAT

The heart is a sin covered by layers of protective innocence and a mask of undis-
covered knowledge

Within each translucent beat radiates a power unmatched by the strength of ten
horses

It surfaces with the smell of sweet perfume or the final steps of a lost love

It can stop without missing a beat or empower you with a feeling of completeness

With each cry of a newborn or the soft sensual touch of a woman's lips, it coats
your senses with impulses of soft rose petals covering the surface of a freshly
planted garden

Awakened to the quiet roar of a heartbeat, a new love is born racing to you in
hopes of finding the path to your heart

Meet Me Halfway

The clouds have parted, awakening a new tomorrow

A ray of light enchants the wave of red flowing through an emotional storm of confusion

The gift is its power

The curse a bond felt by the aching of two hearts

Intoxicated with your beauty within

Drowning in a pool of solitary longing

Nourishment is the only means of survival

Your touch, your breath each hold a key to an escape

Looking into the path guided by your eyes, I see the hope of a new future

All we hear are sounds of silence fill the air as our gaze grows deeper with each moment

Time is now and now is the time

Yesterday, today and tomorrow have a new meaning

Lightning strikes; thunder crashes and rain washes away the fears left behind and provides for a new hope

LAST GOODBYE

Fragile as the wind

Our life but an echo in time planted in the seeds of life for all eternity

A whisper of hello began our slow goodbye

Holding close to a memory locked in the hearts of two

A moment in time sealed away but always alive with the hope of a new tomorrow

Can we begin …

LIFE'S DREAM

Reflections in time mystify a spirituality hovering through the ages of memories lost in painful light above our mortal skies

Searing ahead like a jet without wings

Reaching forward, pulling back

Hiding motionless in a cloud of concrete with nothing beneath but the faith to defy reality

Skin is shedding away all the remorse stricken in the blood flow and dripping from the pores

With all his might he releases the bondages chained up under pillars of flesh and bone

Moving in circles, he turns around only to be stymied by his own progress

With blindness colors grow; life is clear

The path has chosen its master

It's a dream now

Lying on a pillow, birth appears

Soon it is time to open your eyes and awake

EMPTY MIRROR

Kiss my soul

Free my soul

Rape my soul

Forbid me what I cannot have

Drench my spirit with wine from the blood of man

Pillage my temple and leave me with only broken rocks and stones of shattered dreams

Blame me for the sins not yet committed

Convict me for I have not committed a crime

Torture me with unimaginable pain

Crush me deep beneath the ocean

Swallow my existence between white protectors of the skies

I beg for the freedom to fly from this pain covering my body and leave this lifeless form to the infinite voices of hungry spirits roaming inside

A moment to still; a time so right

Where am I

The mirror has no reflection

DREAMING REALITY

Life is a tragic kingdom high above the clouds hovering between reality and fantasy

Decedent dreams send constant reminders of dreams unrealized

Pastels of blue and green paint scenarios of a grinch in a hat and a cat that steals Christmas

We live in a black and white world fogged up by the interpretive dance of uncertainty

Today I died for tomorrow is the first day of a new life

I awaken to the sounds of a new born crying

As I look in the mirror I see myself looking at myself

Crying out loud but only seeing laughter

Through my eyes I see the world for the first time

Reinvented in a time capsule; a destination unknown

All I see is now

All I feel yet unrealized has all been planned in dreams still unperformed.

PROPHECY RETREAT

Gliding through these streets of ruin

Graffiti is the poetry of our lives

Written in a script understood by the music of the young

Lyrics of fear

Chorus of blind hope decorate the foundation of a world forgotten

Tabernacles of icons living and dead are reborn in the underground civilizations

With these walls, we paint

Words, symbols, and signs carefully laid to rest

Sipping nectar of grapes and hiding in our isolated haven, we celebrate

Each day we march; saluting our soldiers

Bowing to our bosses and getting nowhere; each step a retreat

We lease freedom for the price of slavery

Mental pictures snap inside our head

Blinded by reality, they fade into a memory wasteland

Pictures, letters, and dreams burn up an abyss high above the clouds

THE FLAME

My will is gone but not forgotten

Like a runaway train, I am off the tracks and out of control

My soul is a runaway, living on the streets searching for a new meaning

Each sunrise deteriorates the spirit

Under the stars the night protects this fragile pawn naked to a world controlled by neglect and tortured by hatred

Ignite a flame

Re-kindle the light that awakened fondness

Remember the hugs

Remember the smiles

Remember the late night talks and always a clear conscious when your head hit the pillow

The flame burns not for today but for yesterday

It can't return to the comfort it once knew but be comforted by the thoughts represented by the light

I'M SORRY.... FOR WHAT?

Call me something different

Call me something worse than before

Bruise my ego with the same words you used only a pillow length apart

You could have had it

You left the doors on our love

Now you wear this dress for another

Flaunting the beauty of a goddess to the peasant standing before you

I worship you, but now in a different way

A way filled with rocks and glass cutting me and poisoning me with each compliment

I'm sorry

I hate you

I love you

I want you

I want you gone but only if you stay

The picture is only a reminder of the naked passion hidden behind the obvious torture of memories locked in a box in the middle of the ocean floating for a destination far away but always finding its way home

Every goodbye is a new hello

Get off this merry go round that brings me closer to pushing me further away

REST IN FIRENZE

A sea of tranquility echoes silence off the cobblestone

The prayers of the patron saints ring in celebration as church bells chime in peace
faith and harmony

Glasses brimming in wine

Families gather under the warmth of a summer sky

Birds rejoice upon their weekly playground

Strangers become friends and friends, reminders of ourselves

Paintings adorn the faceless walls with reminders of sacrifice

Time disappears into the corners of our mind

As flags of independence and peace point the wind to the sea

Darkness falls over the land

Footsteps escape to the solitude of timeless ruins ushering in the climax of a new
day

HOPE AND FAITH

I woke up today to find that forever is no more

I think about my life and fade to black

The loves lost, the lives lived, the peace only real in the words of the poets

The light of the sun playing hide and seek with millions filled with laughter and tears holding their eyes closed so soon to reveal the passion of the sun's heat

One by one holding hands, blind to color but clear to the awakening spirit eternally grateful for its modest being

Twins are born into a world of confusion and despair

The first is hope and then faith

They crawl toward mountains of castaways looking for their homes

Two cherubs cleansed by the outstretched hands of the eternal lined up along the shore waiting for their collective prayer to be answered

SOCIAL LOVE AFFAIR

On bended knee a union awakens

Hearts flustered with each passing moment of romance like petals in the wind
holding on for a new tomorrow hoping for purity

ODE TO TRAVEL

The modern times of Jack Kerouac

The American spirit of freedom and adventure has transformed itself into self-indulgent laziness when adults have more toys than children. The romanticism of a hand written love letter is now nothing more than an email that may very well have been written by a secretary

Squatting on a train car, with the wind through your hair somewhere between Dayton and Salt Lake, this vast country is full of mystery and intrigue

No schedules, no deadlines, no law except the law of survival

She's sleeping alone with only the clothes on her back

Her dreams packed away in a faded green backpack

She's living the life she wants with the pain she never expected

The sun will rise tomorrow with a new patch of land as her bed

Dreams in repetition as continuous reminders of monotony and realism trapped in the statistics that dictate shifts in lifestyle

TWO WORLDS APART

Her dreams, like sand crystals buried under a golden pond of blue anchored in
the guilt of life

Death has already taken him with each sip of nectar coating the emptiness inside

She runs away, over mountains and streams only to return to herself planted over
the plot of land eternally reserved for guilt stricken self doubt

Shattered over the horizon they stand together defeated in a kiss holding on to
the only thing left undisturbed by time

The pathway to the spirit weakened by the eyes of curiosity and awareness

Light shields him for one more day but darkness awaits its calling

They both wait, backs turned moving further away from the spot they called
home

A new sound grows inside

Whispers the words of tomorrow in a language he will never hear

VALENTINE'S DAY TO AMY

As you lay your head on my shoulders I can feel the presence of your heart beating close to mine

The sweet breath of innocence and purity touch me in silent exhale

The subtle touch of your silky skin massages my inner pain

I am at peace beside your soul; we are one

You are my sun and my moon

You light my days and shield my nights

You protect my fragile being from the fear that rests deep within me

You are the wings that lead my spirit through the air and life my being above the clouds

Hold me tight my precious love

Take my hand and lead me to the place where beauty soars beyond our sweet imagination

GROUNDED

Bitterness hangs in the threshold of the valley of fear

Betrayed by trust and held close by the virtues of the virtuous song of the relic servants of the word

Scriptures bleed on the clothe of the pure spirits flooding the temple of self-doubt

Let the light of inspiration shower flames of mindless abandon into the cave of broken hearts

Hallucinations provide clarity to a world only known by the survivors of the holocaust of terror ringing high above the extended hand of lady liberty

The skies are empty but for a cloud of dust swimming for the freedom of a new tomorrow

Helplessness floating below with signs of salvation elevating from the core of frozen heat

BABY BLUE

Sleeping in a bed of silk, she lays at peace offering a feast of love

She grants access to the angels through the gates of her soul

I watched with humility from a distance caressing the soft curves of her heavenly being with my humbled eyes

Her soothing heart rests now growing inside to shower another day with love

With the pallet of my tongue I taste the fruit of her touch

Soon baby blue will wake

Not a word spoken but only a kiss wetting my lips like the morning rush of the ocean welcoming the land to a new day

The crashing waves explode with each pulse rise

A day yet to begin is now complete holding my baby blue, shelter covers my spirit as the sun ushers through the window

A tear of completeness runs a river from my eye to her heart

THE POET

She sees him in a corner disguised as a poet releasing his inner soul in a steady flow of rhyme

Two worlds collide but never touch

In the distance, only steps away, two children lie under a wilting willow, eyes closed, as the divine power of innocence brings their lips together for the first time

The willow, now the Eiffel Tower on a warm spring night, with their hands joined in a silent endless stare, reach out to the end of the stars

My eyes open now, the dream is over but our fear, still a reality

Across the room, the poet writes with clarity about a dream not realized and a life not yet lived

She feels him calling out for her but for what

Does she feel her lost hope hidden in his words?

Can he release the passion dead in her eyes?

The pen is dried out, the hand rests, and the words are swept off the paper taken by the new rain washing away the days of misery and loneliness

SELF REFLECTION

Shadows hidden from the light beckon a moment of solitary confinement reflecting an image of lucidity cutting through a wall of protection staring at its own enemy

In the middle of a framed portrait of self, words float in the mystical synchronization lining up to castrate memories of successes that are planned on the shelves of your future

Holding up the glass celebrating memories of a better tomorrow

IN FLIGHT

My love is drowning at the bottom of the ocean dried up from the thirsty earth
that is coveting my damaged soul

I fly above the sea of lost dreams spreading my wings as I glide below for a view of
the dark pit I once called happiness

Feathers shed from these damaged wings fighting the winds of destiny for a
chance to recapture the truth

The birds are in the distance now migrating to a new shelter disguised as a warm
solitude of temporary utopia

Dipping our heads into the bitter salts of the waters that blessed the heads of dead
prophets spreading the words through silent prayer

Gliding into the sun now looking for the shelter of a protected future

CRASHING WAVES

The world is covered by pureness

A fresh blanket of white shelters from a winter of darkness

The crescent sun mocks the moon imitating its every move as it unknowingly
sleeps, waiting for the night sky

Nature opens its eyes, breathing life into a new tomorrow

Through absence there is light

Through the depth of daybreak waters rise from the core of the earth rendering
superior prowess on a society intimidated by peace

Solid fortitude of an army of stones smooth from centuries of war, destroy the
gladiators rising from the waters to conquer new lands

Intense heat of frozen tides bubble over, retreating slowly to the abyss

The ghosts of warriors past smile, leaving invisible footsteps on the ground of the
fortress protected once again with the vigor and strength of the human spirit

FROZEN PAST

Shades of blue, purple and green

Thoughts of love, death, hope and fear

Games of trust, heartbreak and greed

One smile,

Life changes, people grow, children are born, friendships emerge, promises made

Hope for a new tomorrow released through the sounds of screaming children on the playground

Love in the radiant glow of a stranger's blue eyes

The sweetness of chocolate

The pureness of fresh sparkling water dripping from the whiteness of a mountaintop

The delicious taste of every reminder of childhood

I saw my dog from eight year old eyes licking my smiling face

He's not here now but his fur still felt on my hands worn down by time

What remains is my aging body hypnotized by the mirror that stops time blinding us of our yesterdays and tomorrows

We are frozen in ourselves, trapped in the body sculpted by divinity and gift wrapped for mortality

I'll pray tonight to the sky and the moon; rain and the stars

For what I don't know

Spirituality is funny that way

TEMPORARY GOODBYE

We say goodbye once again

The sun rising in the east, now sets in the west

Separated from its maternal union held safely in a shelter deep under the horizon

For the beauty of time, we hold on one last time to the memories secured in that
moment with a hug sent down for us to share

Has the will seized?

Has the memory vanished long before the body has found its eternal home?

Shine with me one more time

Remember me for an instant

Dedicate me etched in stone for strangers to walk upon

Looking back I cannot see the past but torn still by the emptiness settled in the
heart of the lonely man on the corner who sees nothing but a cup filled with sym-
pathy of those who visit its home

A gentle tear escapes as the winged eagle lifts itself to the clouded paradise

Looking down through the crowd, a single wave extends to the sky waiting for
the next hello with a smile

"The stars shine above as the world lay to rest with the thoughts of dreams dancing in their heads"

978-0-595-52027-5
0-595-52027-8

Printed in the United States
211639BV00001BA/183/P

9 780595 520275